CW00370079

HOW TO GET YOUR PROSPECT'S ATTENTION
AND KEEP IT!

Magic Phrases
for Network Marketing

KEITH & TOM "BIG AL" SCHREITER

How to Get Your Prospect's Attention and Keep It!
© 2019 by Keith & Tom "Big Al" Schreiter

Published by Fortune Network Publishing
PO Box 890084
Houston, TX 77289 USA

Telephone: +1 (281) 280-9800

BigAlBooks.com

ISBN-10: 1-948197-44-8

ISBN-13: 978-1-948197-44-1

CONTENTS

PREFACE

Prospects are pre-sold.

They want what we have to offer. Let's make a list of what they want.

- Better holidays.
- A way to make their car payments.
- An extra paycheck.
- More energy.
- To work out of their home instead of commuting.
- Younger-looking skin.
- Good health to live longer.
- To pay off their debt.
- Lower utility bills.
- To lose weight.
- Better-tasting, healthier coffee.
- Recognition for their efforts.
- A community of positive people.
- Natural cleaners to help the environment.
- Makeup that makes them look wonderful.
- And, much, much more.

We offer these things in our network marketing businesses.

So, why don't our prospects take advantage of our wonderful offers?

Attention.

They don't hear us. We lose their attention, and their minds drift off to other thoughts. "Oh look! There is a squirrel." With their busy lives, messages, notifications and more, our prospects' attention spans are shorter than ever.

It gets worse.

Even if our prospects focus and listen to our message, they can still block our wonderful offers with their negative programs and filters.

The greatest message in the world is useless if no one hears it.

Let's be heard.

Then our prospects can decide if our message serves them or not.

This book contains magic words and phrases to get our great messages inside our prospects' minds.

- Keith and Tom "Big Al" Schreiter

A LEISURELY WALK EXPLAINS IT ALL.

Two networkers leave their homes for a life-changing walk.

Both joined their companies earlier in the year. They set their goals and created beautiful vision boards on their walls. Both chanted affirmations and sang their company's song. They believe in their company with all of their hearts.

On their individual walks, they met the same stranger.

One networker added a new member to her team. The other distributor talked to the same stranger, but left empty-handed.

What was the difference?

Everything was the same except ... the words they said. The first networker used proven, magic words. The stranger listened and connected with her message, and then joined. The second networker used unproven, ordinary words, and came in second place.

Unfortunately, the second networker didn't know these proven words existed. His untrained words bounced off the stranger's forehead, never entering the prospect's brain. Even the best message is useless if we don't have our prospect's attention.

We have a choice. We can continue to "walk the streets," waste hours on the Internet, buy leads, and come in second place. (There are no company bonuses for second place.)

Or, we can learn proven, magic words, and become network marketing success stories. That sounds and feels a lot better.

What about texting and social media?

Magic words are even more important when texting or on social media. When our prospects can't see our faces, or talk to us "live," how do they judge us?

On the words we use.

Without magic words, they will judge harshly or even ignore us. No second chances.

Simple text messages lack our tone of voice, our facial expressions, our body language, and our natural charisma. Plus, they are easily misunderstood. We don't want to leave our success to chance. Hoping and wishing to be lucky is not a good plan.

So what are magic words for network marketing?

First, these magic words and phrases grab our prospects' attention. Most prospects become unconscious after a few sentences of a boring sales presentation. Their minds drift off to more pleasant thoughts. We naturally filter out sales messages. If no one hears our message, it is over.

Second, these magic words and phrases help us bypass our prospects' filters and barriers to our message. We have a great message to deliver, and we know our message will help our prospects. Unfortunately, our message gets blocked.

Improvised messages bounce off our prospects' foreheads, break up into tiny pieces, and crash to the floor. If our messages never enter our prospects' brains, we have no chance. Our wonderful message encounters their:

- Too-good-to-be-true filter.
- Salesman alarms.
- "What is the catch?" program.
- Negativity.
- Survival programs.
- Skepticism.
- General biases.

We see this happen all the time. Our message seems perfect for our prospects. Our prospects desperately need the benefits we provide. Yes, it is the perfect fit. And then our prospects say "no" to our perfect offer. Ouch!

While this may not appear to make sense on the surface, now we know the problem. Our message never entered our prospects' minds. Those barriers were too much to overcome.

Magic words come to our rescue.

These words and phrases feel more comfortable to our prospects. They help smooth the path for our message to enter their brains.

Think about it. This is all we ask. We want to deliver our message. We want our prospects to hear and understand our message. And then, we allow them to decide whether our message will serve them or not. We don't have to manipulate their decisions. We allow our prospects the freedom to choose.

We can use magic words and phrases everywhere.

- For prospecting.

- For presenting.

- For closing.

- For leading.

- And yes, even for motivating others.

Enough about why we should use magic words. Let's learn some now.

Getting our prospects' attention with magic words.

What is the most important real estate in our prospects' minds?

Attention.

Attention is the new currency.

There is a serious war for our prospects' attention. Advertisements, messages, notifications, interruptions, phone calls, shiny objects, and much, much more dominate our prospects' attention. Everybody wants to dominate and own other people's attention.

We have to bring our prospects' minds to a complete halt, just so they will notice us. If not, we can still talk, but no one is listening. Their blank stares say it all. Our "listener" is thinking other thoughts while we chatter away.

Getting attention for our messages is difficult. Fortunately, we can use magic words to solve this problem. We can be the interesting event that takes our prospects out of their deep hypnotic trance of day-to-day living.

Let's start with an easy phrase that takes control of our prospects' minds.

"I have some good news and some bad news."

Done. We froze our prospects' minds. Nine words.

The survival program and the curiosity program take over when we say these nine words. Our prospects think, "Oh no! This might be important for my survival. I cannot stand the suspense. What is this exciting news I don't know about? Please, please tell me the news."

Now, we can deliver our message to a listening audience.

We don't have to be a psychologist or a levitating superstar to grab our prospects' attention. All we have to do is to say these nine words, "I have some good news and some bad news." This will stun our prospects' minds for about ten seconds while they eagerly await the news. Ten seconds is a long time. We can deliver a huge message in ten seconds.

Now that we own ten seconds of our prospects' attention, what message would we like to deliver? Let's look at some examples.

Imagine that we are talking to a couple. As the conversation drifts to our business, we could rivet their attention with opening words such as these.

Us: "I have some good news and some bad news."

Couple: "What? Give us the bad news first, please."

Us: "The bad news is that no matter how hard we work at our jobs, we will never have enough money to retire. The laws of math make that impossible. The good news is that a second income makes it easy."

Couple: "So how do we get a second income?"

Our couple went from drifting minds on autopilot to interested prospects. They want to know how to get a second income. How long did this take? Seconds.

How about this?

Us: "I have some good news and some bad news."

Couple: "Oh my! What is the news?"

Us: "The good news is that with this business, we can work out of our home 24 hours a day. The bad news is that we will miss our boss and fellow employees at our current jobs."

Couple: "No problem. We can live with that. Tell us more about your business."

Is the couple open-minded now? Yes. Instead of looking for reasons why our business **won't** work for them, they now look for reasons why our business **will** work for them. These ten seconds changed their attitude toward the rest of our message. We avoided the negative experience of presenting our business to skeptical critics. We created a positive-minded audience.

Did we notice that it did not matter if we put the good news first or the bad news first? When we use these nine words, we freeze our prospects' brains. So, it doesn't matter which we choose to say first.

What if we ask our prospects, "Which news would you like to hear first?" They will want to hear the bad news first. Humans are wired to look for bad news. We want to survive. We want to know if there is any bad news on the horizon that might affect our survival.

Can our prospects resist this brain freeze?

No. It is almost unfair.

Sure, they could pretend to not want to know the news, but what will they be thinking about every time they review our conversation? They will be thinking, "I wonder what was the good news and what was the bad news."

These nine magic words are easy to use. Let's warm up our creativity muscles now with a few more sample conversations.

Us: "I have some good news and some bad news."

Couple: "Just a moment. Let's turn down the TV volume. What is the news?"

Us: "The bad news is that car insurance, medical costs, and taxes keep rising but our paychecks don't. But the good news is that we can start a part-time business and start getting the big-time tax deductions that large businesses get. That can help us a lot."

Couple: "That sounds good, but doesn't that take a big investment?"

Us: "More good news. We can start a part-time business with no overhead and almost no start-up costs."

Couple: "Wait a moment. Let's turn off the TV. We want to talk now."

Our prospects volunteered their undivided attention by offering to turn off the TV. That is a great sign.

Us: "I have some good news and some bad news."

Couple: "What is the news?"

Us: "The bad news is that we are going to die. But the good news is that this product will help us delay that event as long as possible."

Couple: "Oh my! Tell us about this product."

***

Us: "I have some good news and some bad news."

Co-worker: "I can handle bad news. I work here at the same dreary job that you do. So tell me, what is this bad news?"

Us: "The bad news is that the boss wants us to work overtime on Saturday again, so he will get a bigger bonus at the end of the year. He is building a big house for his retirement. But the good news is that I found someone who could help us start a part-time business and give us an escape plan. I am having coffee with her tomorrow. Do you want to join me?"

Co-worker: "Absolutely! I have to start doing something for my life instead of the boss's life."

Attention.

As we can see, attention is everything. If prospects don't hear our message, nothing happens. It doesn't matter how good our message is.

What grabs the attention of our prospects? Something different. Something out of the ordinary. For most of our lives, we walk around on autopilot. Only when something seems out of place do we take notice.

Do we perk up when we hear the doorbell? When lightning flashes? When a giant monster walks into the room? (Okay, slightly exaggerated.)

So when we say we have some good news, our prospects think, "That is different. I should pay attention."

And when we say we have some bad news, our prospects think, "That is new. That sounds ominous. I'm worried about my survival. I should pay attention."

To capture our prospects' attention, we should think, "Big, bold, new, unusual, exciting, unexpected, different." People have naturally short attention spans. We can't expect that to change. We must adjust our words to get their attention.

It is easy to quiet our prospects' minds so that they will hear our message. These nine words, "I have some good news and some bad news," do the job quickly.

Once our prospects are listening, then we can insert our problems and solutions into our "good news/bad news" conversation. Our prospects hear our message loud and clear. They will determine if our message will be of service to them or not.

Is this the only nine-word combination in the history of humanity?

Of course not. The beauty of magic words and phrases is that there are so many to choose from. The more we know, the easier it is to get our message heard.

When we first discover how easy this is, we think of all the prospects we ruined in the past. We can't change our past. But we can take action and design our future. We want to give every prospect a chance to hear our message loud and clear.

So what is another nine-word phrase that we could use?

"There are two types of people in the world."

Again we freeze our prospects' minds. Nine words.

The survival program and the curiosity program again take over when we say these nine words. Our prospects think, "Oh no! This might be important for my survival. S-h-h-h-h. I can't stand the suspense. Plus, I wonder what the two different types are? And which type am I?"

Now we can deliver our message to an attentive audience. They are like puppies waiting for a treat. Wagging tails, drooling, full attention.

Don't believe that these words work? Try this.

In a conversation, say, "There are two types of people in the world." Then, say nothing else. And wait. And wait. The suspense will drive our conversation partners crazy.

Now is a good time to have some fun. Here are some examples of saying these nine words and including our message with them.

"There are two types of people in the world. Those who try to get by on one paycheck every month, and those who know how to get a second check."

Our prospects can choose which group they want to be in. They can continue their lives as they are. Or, they can raise their hands and volunteer by saying, "Hey, tell me more. How do I get a second paycheck?"

Did we notice that all we did was give our prospects an option? They could ignore our option, or volunteer to take the option. No rejection. Comfortable for everyone. Let's do some more.

"There are two types of families in the world. Those that take ordinary vacations, and those that take vacations that they will remember forever."

What do you think the next words will be from our prospects? Most prospects will open up their minds and ask us, "How does that work?"

This might seem too easy. But getting people to open their minds with magic words is simple to master in minutes. Here are more of these opening magic statements.

"There are two types of dieters in the world. Those who eat funny foods, exercise, starve themselves, and watch the weight keep coming back. And, those who lose weight one time and keep it off forever."

"There are two types of people in the world. Those who have a lawyer on speed-dial, and those who get taken advantage of."

"There are two types of people in the world. Those who struggle to stay awake in the afternoon at work, and those who have energy the entire day."

"There are two types of people in the world. Those who try to fix their wrinkles by putting creams and lotions on top of their skin, and those who fix their wrinkles with good nutrition from the inside."

"There are two types of people in the world. Those who use cheap makeup and cosmetics, and those who want to look their best every day of their life."

"There are two types of people in the world. Those who use chemical cleaners in their homes, and those who care about the environment and use natural cleaners instead."

"There are two types of people in the world. Those who fight traffic every day to and from work, and those who enjoy working out of their homes."

"There are two types of people in the world. Those who want to do something for their health, and those who give up and don't care."

"There are two types of students in the world. Those who graduate with huge student debt, and those who graduate with a part-time business that pays off their student loans."

"There are two types of homeowners in the world. Those who pay too much for their utilities, and those who get extra savings that can help them pay off their mortgages."

"There are two types of women in the world. Those who go to their high school reunion looking 20 years older, and those who make all their classmates jealous."

"There are two types of drivers in the world. Those who stress out every time they go slightly over the speed limit, and those who know the secret to getting out of tickets."

"There are two types of people in the world. Those who pay retail for their utility bills, and those who take the automatic discount every month."

"There are two types of people in the world. Those who enjoy high cellphone bills, and those who get better service for less."

"There are two types of people in the world. Those who complain about money, and those who know how to get more." (Guess what our prospects will say next.)

PROSPECTS JUDGE US ... HARSHLY.

We only get one chance to make a great first impression. Our first words can make a huge difference. Choosing good words to start a conversation with prospects gives us the best chance to make a favorable impression.

Our magic words should be safe. No need to alarm or insult our prospects. We don't want to invite rejection. When we have good relationships with prospects, good things happen.

This doesn't have to be complicated. For example, here is a two-word sequence that helps freeze our prospects' brains, so we can deliver our message.

"Guess what?"

What is the most common response we would expect from this phrase?

"I don't know, what?"

And now our prospects' minds await our message. Here are a few examples.

Us: "Guess what?"

Prospects: "What?"

Us: "We can now lose weight while eating all the chocolate we want."

Now we wait for the reaction and answer. If our prospects like chocolate, and want to lose weight, they pre-sell themselves before we even begin our next sentence. They might be thinking, "Here is all my money. Bring on the chocolate!"

Us: "Guess what?"

Prospects: "Uh, I don't know. What?"

Us: "I started to use a new facial serum last week, and my husband can see the difference already. My wrinkles are shrinking."

If our prospects worry about their wrinkles, they will volunteer and say, "That sounds awesome. Tell me more." Their minds make a decision to try something new.

All we have to do is take the volunteers. If someone is not interested, they can change the subject. Here are a few more quick ones.

Us: "Guess what?"

Prospects: "Go ahead."

Us: "I got my insurance premiums to go down. Now I have more money for our weekend family activities."

***

Us: "Guess what?"

Prospects: "Tell us."

Us: "I am going to start my own business, but with no risk. I will start part-time to be safe."

***

Us: "Guess what?"

Prospects: "I give up. What?"

Us: "I am going to start a new career. Working here is not my future."

***

Us: "Guess what?"

Prospects: "What?"

Us: "I got my first bonus check from my part-time business. I'm going to use it to pay off some bills."

***

Us: "Guess what?"

Prospects: "Uh, we give up. What's new?"

Us: "I can get wholesale vacations now, so our family can take a big-time holiday for cheap."

Two words. Instant attention. Open-minded prospects. No harsh selling. No rejection. All we have to do is take the volunteers who connect with our message.

Now, these magic words are starting to make sense.

Humans have lazy brains. What do prospects do when we talk to them? They listen for a few key words, make a quick decision on those words, and then drift off to think about something else. That is how we get judged so quickly.

An easy way to illustrate this is to look at the anatomy of a phone call asking our friend for an appointment. Let's look at the words we use, and what our friend is thinking based upon those words.

Caution, this might be painful.

Us: "Hi good friend."

Friend: (Uh-oh. You are going to ask me for a favor. I hope you don't ask me for a loan. Or ask me to move furniture. I hate moving furniture.)

Us: "I just joined a brand-new business ..."

Friend: (Oh no. This is not going to end well. You will ask me to buy something or do something I don't want to do. How do I get out of this?)

Us: "And would love to give you a presentation."

Friend: (A presentation? Salesman alarm! Looks like you will be pitching me something for an hour and will make me feel bad if I don't buy or join. I hate presentations.)

Us: "I only need 30 minutes of your time."

Friend: (30 minutes? I don't even have 30 seconds. I have thousands of other decisions I have to manage. I can't stop my life for some sales pitch to buy other people's stuff.)

Us: "When would be a good time to come by? Tuesday at 2 PM or Thursday at 4 PM?"

Friend: (Did an alien take over your body? You don't talk like that. You sound like some sleazy salesman from a cheap 1970s movie.)

This gets worse, but we don't want to go there. Nobody wants extra nightmares while they sleep.

Did we notice that certain words trigger bad feelings in our brains?

If certain words have the power to make our brains say "no," then certain words have the power to make our brains say "yes."

So the question we should ask ourselves is, "If I am going to talk anyway, which words should I use? Should I use the words that get 'no' decisions, or should I use the words that get 'yes' decisions?"

We don't have to be rocket scientists to answer this question. But isn't it great to know that certain words and phrases work, and that we have the power to choose these words?

Ready for some more short magic phrases?

"Well, you know how ..."

What a great way to introduce our business or products into the conversation. Our prospects hear these words every day from others. For example, imagine we are at the coffee machine at work. Our colleagues start complaining as usual. They say things such as:

"Well, you know how bad the traffic is on Highway 201 every day?"

"Well, you know how the company provides us with free coffee that tastes awful?"

"Well, you know how it always rains on weekends?"

"Well, you know how this job takes up most of our week?"

Everyone hears these words daily. They don't even pay attention to these words when they hear them. These words are part of the noise we ignore every day. But when we say these words, our prospects want to believe whatever we say next. I talk more about this in our book, *How To Get Instant Trust, Belief, Influence and Rapport! 13 Ways To Create Open Minds By Talking To The Subconscious Mind.*

Here is the good part. When we say these four words, our listeners start nodding and smiling almost immediately. And that is before they even hear the end of our sentence! This is one of the safest phrases to introduce our business and products into a social situation. Here are a few more examples of using this phrase to start conversations in the right direction.

"Well, you know how hard it is to get ahead now?"

"Well, you know how we want to live longer?"

"Well, you know how we want our face to be our best first impression?"

"Well, you know how exercise interferes with our week?"

"Well, you know how tired we get in the afternoons?"

"Well, you know how weekends are so much fun?"

When we use this phrase, our listeners feel great. Whatever we say next feels familiar. We create rapport and a great conversation.

This is one of the easiest sets of magic words to practice. Insert these words in front of your favorite sayings, and watch how people relax. After doing this for a week, we are on our way to making it a habit.

"This may or may not be your cup of tea, but ..."

Back in the 1970s, I attended a workshop to learn new techniques for my network marketing business. The instructor, John Walker, said, "Make it easy and rejection-free when you talk to people. Give them a natural escape so if they are not interested, they won't feel embarrassed. In return, they will be polite to you."

That sounded great. I hated rejection. A perfect solution for shy introverts like me. When we give prospects a way to graciously say "no" to us, they don't have to make up phony objections like, "It is a pyramid. I need to research this for a while. I have to ask the squirrels in my backyard first."

He continued by instructing us to say, "This may or may not be your cup of tea, but ..."

And wow! These magic words made prospecting easier. Now I could say things such as:

"This may or may not be your cup of tea, but I recently started a new business. I thought you might be interested also."

"This may or may not be your cup of tea, but I just found a way to start a part-time business that won't interfere with my job. Is this something you would like to check out also?"

"This may or may not be your cup of tea, but I am giving up commuting and going to work from my home. Do you hate commuting also?"

"This may or may not be your cup of tea, but have you ever thought about being your own boss?"

"This may or may not be your cup of tea, but I think I might know where we could make a lot of money."

"This may or may not be your cup of tea, but this is something that could help us retire early."

Here is what happened when I used this phrase. Most of the prospects would say, "Tell me more." Now I had someone with a more open mind to hear my message. And everyone felt good. That was important.

If "cup of tea" is not a familiar idiom where you live, you can substitute, "This may or may not be interesting to you, but ..."

Here are some quick examples.

"This may or may not be interesting to you, but I found a way to sleep better at night."

"This may or may not be interesting to you, but Mary told me a great way to lose weight fast."

"This may or may not be interesting to you, but now we can travel and get great discounts."

"This may or may not be interesting to you, but I have a product that turns back time on our faces."

"The trap."

"Trap" conjures up all types of negative emotions in our brains. This is a famous headline formula that gets attention:

"The _____ trap."

Here are examples to prime our creativity.

- The job trap.

- The commuting trap.

- The wrinkling trap.

- The diet trap.

- The "holiday from hell" trap.

- The retirement trap.

- The daycare trap.

- The retirement savings trap.

The "scam" word brings the same effect. It isn't hard to engage listeners and readers.

"Controversy!"

A controversial statement or headline stands out. We give it our attention.

What are some controversial statements that would shock our prospects?

- Exercise is overrated.

- Fruit is bad for your health.

- Savings accounts are obsolete.

- Responsibility stress causes men to die early.

- Cars should be outlawed.

- Pimples are good for us.

Once we have their attention, we explain why we started with these words. They will listen to our message. Here is an example.

"Stop over-educating your children!"

"Science proves that the biggest factor for success is action. Replacing action with education only prepares our children for low-level, mindless jobs, working for the people who took action in their lives. It is often said that 'A' students in school end up working for the 'C' students in school who started their own businesses."

Why are all these phrases so simple?

Because our brains are lazy. We love to make automatic decisions based upon what we know. Our subconscious mind stores these decisions for us.

However, if we get a lot of new information or challenges, this will require hard work by our conscious mind. Our brain doesn't like that.

Sure, we would like to think that we consciously think through all of our decisions. Unfortunately, that is not true. To conserve our precious brain energy, we use shortcuts.

When our brain is challenged with something new, it tries to relate it to something that it can decide automatically. It often changes the question just to make it easy. Here is an example.

A salesman gives a long and complicated presentation. Lots of information, videos, and too many choices. Our brains can do two things.

#1. Carefully think through all the information. Consider the consequences of the choices. Wow. That is going to be a lot of work, and take a lot of time. But, we have thousands more decisions waiting for our brain. Now we feel stressed.

Or,

#2. Re-frame this entire salesman encounter as a simpler question. "Do I like and trust salespeople?" That creates a quick and automatic "no" answer. Excellent! That was much easier. Now, on to those other decisions I have waiting, such as what I should watch on television tonight.

This is why we must keep everything simple.

The smarter strategy is to grab our prospects' attention and deliver a short, clear message. That is kinder to our prospects' brains.

But we are just getting started. What else can we say to grab our prospects' attention?

Presenting with magic words.

It is great to capture our prospects' attention, but it is another challenge to keep it.

Our prospects get bored fast. We have to constantly re-engage them with magic phrases throughout our presentation. That means we need a variety of ways to get them to think, "Hey! I need to pay attention to what you say next."

Most of these magic phrases work any time. We can use them at the beginning, middle, or end of our presentation. All we want is for our prospects to hear our great message.

Let's do some quick and easy magic phrases.

"Don't take my word for it."

Prospects are skeptical. Why shouldn't they be? Everyone is trying to sell them something, manipulate them, influence them, and push an agenda everywhere they go. So how do we break through the skepticism? We can shock them into consciousness by saying, "Don't take my word for it."

This keeps prospects from judging us and our credibility. Our prospects will think, "So whose word should I take for this fact? I feel better about getting proof from an outside source or a third party." Here are a few ways to use this in real-life situations.

"Don't take my word for it. Look at your own experience." (Hopefully our prospect's personal experience will verify that what we are saying is true.)

"Don't take my word for it. Look at what the experts are saying."

"Don't take my word for it that this is a great opportunity. Instead, look at the proof. The company offers a 100% money-back guarantee. They wouldn't be doing that if they were not confident of your success."

"Don't take my word for it. In 30 days, look into the mirror and see the proof for yourself."

"Don't take my word for it. Let's go on the Internet right now and see what others have to pay for their travel compared to our special discount price."

"Don't take my word for it. The government lists all the harmful ingredients we should be avoiding."

"Don't take my word for it. Identify the worst skin problems you have, and see what this cream can do in only four days."

This is a great way to fight our prospects' natural skepticism.

"But here is an even better idea."

"A better idea? That sounds exciting! What is this better idea you speak of?"

What a great way to re-engage our prospects' attention. Maybe we buried our prospects in facts, features and benefits. That is mind-numbing. We are talking about our stuff, and not about our prospects. This simple phrase alerts our prospects that we are about to say something new and interesting. They want to hear it.

Some examples?

"But here is an even better idea. Instead of having your current breakfast add to your waistline, drink our weight-loss shake for breakfast. Now your breakfast will be making you thinner every day."

"But here is an even better idea. Instead of extreme budgeting, why not enjoy the luxury of a second paycheck every month?"

"But here is an even better idea. Instead of fighting wrinkles on the outside with creams and lotions, fight the cause of wrinkles from the inside."

"But here is an even better idea. Instead of showing your children pictures of Disney World, take them to Disney World! How? By creating a second income with our travel business."

"But here is an even better idea. Instead of spending hours volunteering for trash pickup to help the environment, switch to natural cleaning products in your home. This will have a more lasting effect than a one-time cleanup."

"But here is an even better idea. Pay for your child's college education with a part-time business. Then your child will graduate with no student loans."

"But here is an even better idea. Instead of lecturing the children to turn off the lights, simply allow us to send you a lower electricity bill."

"Consider this."

This almost sounds like a command. But when we say, "Consider this," our prospects immediately pay attention.

To them, they are about to receive an offer. Or, they are going to hear about something that will pay off in their future.

Let's take a look at a few examples.

"Consider this. We can extend our lives with carefully-planned nutrition."

"Consider this. Company jobs aren't as secure as they used to be, and we want the financial security of a second paycheck."

"Consider this. Wrinkles happen. Now we can do something about those wrinkles."

"Consider this. Dieting doesn't work. We have to be smarter than that."

"Consider this. We can never retire while working a job. There isn't enough salary money to go around."

"Consider this. Vacations should create family memories. This program shows us how to take family vacations at a discounted price."

"Consider this. Commuting is wasted time that we will never get back."

If we use "consider this" with our prospects, they will listen to our next few sentences.

"Which means."

"Which means" is an excellent phrase to explain our jargon and technical words. This helps our prospects understand what we're talking about. When we say "group volume," our prospects won't understand what we mean. So we expand on our message with the words, "which means." Here are two quick examples.

We could say, "We get paid on our group volume, which means, the sales of all the people we sponsor, and the people they sponsor, etc."

Or, "We use the latest liposome technology, which means our product goes directly into our cells for maximum potency."

"Which means" is a powerful way to explain hard-to-understand terms. But there is a bigger benefit.

"Which means" grabs our prospects' attention. When they hear these words, they think, "An explanation is coming. This will help me understand. I should pay attention."

This "which means" phrase will take them out of their daydreaming mode and grab their attention. Let's do some examples.

"In our business, you get a sponsor, which means you have an experienced person to help you get started."

"Our products work fast, which means your customers will see immediate results and smile."

"You can create a part-time income with us, which means you can pay off your credit card debt faster."

"With our diet program, all you do is change your breakfast, which means you won't have to starve yourself."

"This business is simple, which means I can explain it to you in only two minutes."

"This business can grow, which means you can eventually work out of your home instead of commuting."

"You can call our lawyers in an emergency, which means you never have to worry about someone taking advantage of you."

"Our products are natural, which means you will be improving the environment every time you use them."

"Which means" is a powerful way to re-engage our prospects so that they hear our message.

"For example."

Our brains like simple concepts. We don't want to think too hard.

How do we signal to our prospects that we are about to simplify things for them? With the words, "for example."

Saying the words "for example" will renew our prospects' attention in our conversation.

Here are some examples.

"For example, let's say that you continue at your job until you are 65. Do you think you will have enough retirement savings for another 20 or 30 years?"

"For example, most household cleaners are full of chemicals. They damage our waterways."

"For example, you learned to use a smartphone, so you have the ability to learn the skills of our business."

"For example, suppose that you are stopped by the police, and the situation takes a turn for the worse. This membership allows you to instantly get an attorney on the phone."

"For example, even if you get a 5% raise this year, it won't keep up with inflation."

"For example, if everyone in the office worked harder, only the boss would get a bigger house for his retirement."

"For example, this protein shake replaces your normal expensive and fattening breakfast. This makes it easy to lose weight."

"For example, most wrinkles begin at age 30, but smart people know how to delay them."

"For example, this small pill replaces the nutrition of 2 pounds of lettuce."

"For example, my sister used this travel membership and saved $300 off the lowest price on the Internet."

Our prospects love examples.

"Do you ever have the feeling that something isn't quite right?"

Sounds like a beginning to a horror movie, doesn't it? Well, it is a great hook to get people's attention.

What comes next? A story, of course.

Now our prospects will listen to our message.

Not good with micro-stories? Don't worry. Create the story around:

- Skepticism.

- Doubt.

- Our prospects' problems.

Here are a few examples.

"Do you ever have the feeling that something isn't quite right? So there I was, 40 years old, with 20 years of working behind me. And what did I have to show for my 20 years of hard work? Mortgage payments, car payments, and no money in my savings account. And I'm thinking, 'This isn't right. I need to make a change.' And that is why I looked at this part-time business."

What are our prospects thinking after hearing our micro-story? Many will visualize themselves in that story. They will want to know more about what we did next to change things.

Here is another micro-story.

"Do you ever have the feeling that something isn't quite right? When we were young, we could eat huge junk food meals and stay skinny. Now, all we have to do is look at a french fry and we gain weight. So I figured out dieting and starving wouldn't fix this problem, but changing my metabolism would. Now I can eat and not gain all that extra weight."

And another.

"Do you ever have the feeling that something isn't quite right? We look at our electricity bills, and we know they are overcharging us somehow, but we don't know how they are doing it. I sort that out for people so they get a lower electricity bill. No use overpaying when we don't have to."

And one more.

"Do you ever have the feeling that something isn't quite right? Some people wrinkle a lot, and others don't seem to wrinkle at all. What do those non-wrinklers know that we don't know? So I went to a seminar to discover their secret."

Ah, this is too much fun. Remember this quote by Ellen Goodman? She doesn't use the words, "Do you ever have the feeling that something isn't right?" But we could put them in front of this quote and it would sound completely natural.

"Normal is getting dressed in clothes that you buy for work and driving through traffic in a car that you are still paying for, in order to get to the job you need to pay for the clothes and the car, and the house you leave vacant all day so you can afford to live in it."

We are only starting on these attention-grabbing phrases. Ready for more?

"THERE IS A CATCH."

Take control of our prospects' minds. Simply say these four words: "There is a catch."

Survival is the #1 program that runs our lives. Our minds run that program first to make sure that we survive. If we don't survive, well, then nothing else matters. When we tell our prospects that there is a catch, they clear their minds of all thoughts. Then, they concentrate on what we are about to say next. What a great opportunity to deliver our message.

The good news is that if we expose a "catch" in our presentation, it gives us credibility. Everybody knows that nothing is perfect. When we tell our prospects that our offer is not perfect, they tend to believe us more. To them, it appears that we are giving them a fair and unbiased presentation.

But the primary reason to say that there is a catch is to get our message inside our prospects' heads. Again, our goal is to have our message heard, and then let our prospects decide if our message will serve them or not.

Time for some examples.

"Yes, you can earn a lot of extra money with our business. However, there is a catch. You will end up paying more income taxes also."

"Our skincare system will make your skin look younger and younger every month. But, there is a catch. If you use it too long, you will look too young to buy alcohol at your favorite bar."

"Eventually, you can do our business full-time out of your home. This sounds good, but there is a catch. You will miss your boss and fellow employees at your former job."

"Our super-nutrition package turns back the hands of time. It can even work for your grandmother. But, there is a catch. Your grandmother will be asking you for rides to her karate lessons and her break-dancing performances."

"You can earn more in your business than you can at your job. But there is a catch. It could take several months of no income to lay the foundation of your new business."

"There is a catch" is a powerful way to get the attention of our prospects.

"But here is the problem ..."

Similar to "There is a catch," this phrase grabs our prospects' attention. Problems are ten times more interesting to prospects than benefits. Our negative biases love to focus on problems. All we have to do is to attach our offer to this phrase.

"But here is the problem. To get extra money, we have to work two or even three jobs. And there are only 24 hours in a day. The solution is to start a part-time business. This business can grow while we work a full-time job."

"But here is the problem. Dieting makes us hungry. This makes us miserable. So instead, let's change what we eat and let our healthy shakes naturally take off that extra weight."

"But here is the problem. Getting a lawyer to protect our rights requires large retainer fees. With our service, we can talk to a lawyer 24 hours a day by phone for one low monthly membership fee."

"But here is the problem. Our skincare system will make you look younger in just 30 days. However, your friends at work will feel jealous."

"But here is the problem. It is easy to get discouraged while building our part-time business. That is why we recommend 15 minutes of personal development every day."

"But here is the problem. We have skills for a different profession. Now we are starting a new profession with network marketing. We will have to take time to learn the new skills."

"If you don't …"

The FOMO (Fear Of Missing Out) program works overtime in our prospects' brains. They don't want the regret of not taking advantage of an opportunity.

But there is an opposing fear, the fear of making a bad choice.

Which fear is stronger in prospects?

The fear of making a bad choice.

To overcome our prospects' fear of making a bad choice, we will focus on what they might lose by not moving forward with us. How do we do that?

Try asking this question at the appropriate time:

"So if you don't start a part-time business, then what will happen?"

This gives our prospects a chance to think of the bad things that will happen if they don't get extra money. Maybe they see their current bills piling up. Or they might have to choose an inferior school for the children.

Once they see this grim picture, they become more open-minded about our opportunity.

Instead of looking for reasons why our business won't work, they start looking for reasons why our business will work.

Rory Williams suggested this when talking to graduating college students. She says, "If you don't start a part-time business, how are you going to chisel away at your college debt and still build your career?"

So what will they think? "Wow! You are right. I have this huge college debt that is a dark cloud over my next 10 or 15 years. I want to get rid of that cloud so I can get on with my dream life. So tell me how this would work." Instant engagement.

Here are some more examples.

> "If you continue to try to pay all your bills with your one monthly paycheck, what will that look like in the future?"

> "If you don't start on this diet program today, where do you think you will be in 30 days?"

> "If you don't have this legal plan to protect you, do you think that the people taking advantage of you will have mercy on you?"

> "If you don't take advantage of our discount travel program, how much will you spend on your next holiday?"

"If you don't stop the wrinkling from the inside, do you think the wrinkling will stop on its own?"

"If you don't start a part-time business now, how will you get the money to invest for your retirement?"

"If you don't start building your own business now, how much longer can you put up with your dream-sucking, vampire boss?"

"If you decide not to start a business to work out of your home now, do you think you will somehow start to enjoy your two hours of commuting every day?"

"A word of caution ..."

You guessed it. This phrase works similar to the previous phrase. People hate making mistakes, so they will hear our every word. Here are some examples.

"A word of caution. Our weight-loss system is so rapid that you might want to do it under the supervision of your family doctor."

"A word of caution. When the bonus checks come in, many people go out and buy new toys. Instead, we recommend paying down any debt first."

"A word of caution. Having a personal lawyer on autodial makes one feel powerful and might go to one's head."

"A word of caution. These organic cleaners are concentrated. Only use 25% of what you normally do."

"A word of caution. Losing two hours a day commuting in traffic can never be recovered. You need a different plan."

"A word of caution. We are not getting any younger, so let's at least slow down our aging process."

"It gets worse."

Oh no! What happens next? How bad can it be?

If we want to increase the drama and tension in our prospects' minds, these words work. We will have their attention. That means our next words will be heard. Some quick examples.

"It gets worse. Prices go up 10 to 20% every year. Our paycheck only goes up 1%."

"It gets worse. Most ordinary vacations can be stressful. We come back feeling more tired than when we left."

"It gets worse. When we starve ourselves to lose weight, our metabolism slows down. This makes it even harder to lose weight."

"It gets worse. When we are finally old enough to retire, we are too old to enjoy it."

"It gets worse. They are not building any new roads, so commuting will take longer every year."

"It gets worse. Wrinkles are a one-way road. Once we get them, we can't get rid of them."

Bad news is the easiest way to get our prospects' attention.

"Now."

Our brains are pretty basic. They make decisions based upon programs developed through generations and generations of humanity.

People like to stay within their comfort zones. This explains why people prefer to stay where they are. They know what their experience will be. Doing something new takes them outside of their comfort zones. We hesitate to risk those new experiences.

Also, the future is hard for our brains to visualize. Our brains understand the "now." So when we talk about the future, we may stress our prospects' brains. When we talk about the "now," it is easy for our brains to understand and visualize.

Want some examples of how "now" is easy, and the future is hard for us to plan?

- Life insurance. People hate to buy life insurance. They have to be sold.

- Healthy diets. We eat cake and ice cream now and don't worry about tomorrow.

- Exercise? We will start that exercise program later.

- Work now, and wait to get paid in the future? Now, that is going to be hard for people to visualize.

One way to relieve stress is to focus our presentation on the "now."

If we can get our prospects to think about an immediate step, they won't think too hard about what they have to do in the future. Our strategy is to lay out a simple, first step for our prospects.

Ask ourselves, "What kinds of first steps can I propose to our prospects that feel simple and easy for them to execute?"

Here are some examples of "now" first steps for our prospects.

"Let's mix up a protein shake now. Taste it. Then repeat this every morning for two weeks. We will talk then."

"Put this cream on your face now. Then, feel the difference tomorrow morning when you wake up."

"Let's get you registered for training now. We can do the rest of the paperwork later."

"Look at this brochure of holidays now. Pick a holiday that you want to take with your family."

Our brains make quick "now" decisions. We hate going through information, videos, flipcharts, testimonials, research reports, lists of ingredients, etc. Instead, our brains make quick "yes" and "no" decisions and ignore the information.

So having fewer fine details, making things simple, and keeping our conversation in the "now" makes it easier for our prospects to go ahead with a "yes" decision.

"Now" is always better than sometime in the future.

"Free!"

The word "free" seems to short-circuit our brains. We love "free."

Salesman: "Experience our free five-day trial. Then you can decide."

Our minds: "Be careful. There must be a catch. But, the salesman said it was free. What could go wrong? We love free. But shouldn't we be skeptical? But free means there is no risk. Well, maybe we should say that we want to think it over to be safe. But it is free, so why don't we take advantage of it right away? Free is good. Free! Free! Free!"

Yes, there is something about the word "free" that gets us into action immediately. When we use this word with our prospects, their desire for "free" overcomes much of their resistance. Here are some examples of using the word "free" in our conversations.

"Use this free sample so you can experience the benefits."

"Our free five-day trial means you have time before making your final decision."

"Join us on our free training call on Tuesday night. You will love the tips."

"Our regular customers get free bonus products every month."

"Free look at our business on Tuesday night at 7 PM."

"Free training when you join our business tonight."

"Free trips paid by the company!"

"You" and "We/Us."

Humans are selfish. We think about ourselves a lot. In our opinion, the universe revolves around us. Take a quick look at a group picture. Who do we look for first? Ourselves, of course.

When we talk to our prospects, we should keep this selfish tendency in mind. Our prospects don't care about us, and they care even less about what we have to offer.

When we talk to others, here are two strategies that work.

Strategy #1: Use the word "you" a lot. This helps us focus on our prospects, and not on our stuff. We want to talk about our prospects' business, our prospects' problems, etc. This is all our prospects are interested in. Now is a good time to check ourselves by recording one of our conversations. If we hear that we use the "I" word too frequently, now is the time to change how we talk to our prospects.

Examples?

Before: "I have this great product."

After: "You can have this great product."

Before: "I can solve this problem."

After: "You can solve this problem."

Before: "I represent ..."

After: "This is for you ..."

Before: "Our product is great."

After: "You will love this."

When we speak to others, the conversation should be all about them.

Strategy #2: Use "We/Us" to make our prospects feel more comfortable. They might start to feel like they are part of a team. When our prospects have to make decisions and take action alone, the fear of change slows them down. When we offer to hold their hands through this process, it is easier for them to move forward. And as a bonus, it helps us build stronger rapport.

Here are some examples.

Before: "You can start tonight."

After: "We can start tonight."

Before: "You hate the long commute to the job."

After: "We hate commuting."

Before: "Dieting is difficult."

After: "We find dieting hard to do with our busy lives."

Before: "This product helps reduce wrinkles."

After: "We can use this product to reduce our wrinkles."

"Slipped by me like a Vaseline-coated ninja at midnight."

Twenty years ago, I was bouncing up and down on a cruise ship near Antarctica. Bored. So I decided to surf the Internet to pass the time and challenge Art Jonak to a headline-writing experiment. I had the time to plot my perfect headline for engagement.

On our forum, I posted, "Slipped by me like a Vaseline-coated ninja at midnight." The headline rocked. Blew everything else away in the forum … except for Art's headline. He simply posted, "Here is proof!"

I don't know why, but when we announce that we have proof, people engage. Maybe people think, "I wasn't sure before, but hey, here is proof. This must be good! Let's see if I agree."

To grab our prospects' attention, all we have to say is, "Here is proof!" Our prospects desperately want to read or hear our proof.

"Here is proof!" works well to get our prospects' attention on social media.

Here are some examples.

"You won't be hungry on this diet. Here is proof!"

"To all my skeptics, here is proof!"

"Here is proof! Your skin will look younger in just four days."

"You will never be able to retire. Here is proof!"

"Yes, we can extend our lives. Here is proof!"

"We don't need a college degree to be rich. Here is proof!"

These three simple words make it easy to get prospects to listen to us.

Now, let's look at more magic phrases that we can use.

HAVE A CONVERSATION INSTEAD OF A PRESENTATION.

Having a conversation means allowing our prospects to talk. To make our conversations interesting, our prospects should do most of the talking. How do we make that happen? With questions.

Our fact-filled presentations are boring. Prospects see hundreds of advertisements every week. To them, they are all a blur. Everyone claims to be the first, the best, the biggest, and the most wonderful thing that has ever happened in the history of humanity. Prospects feel immune to the hype.

Presentations don't get prospects to make decisions anyway, so let's not worry about them. Instead, let's focus the conversation we can have with prospects to lead them to decisions. This is where professionals spend their time.

Here are some questions we can ask that help lead our prospects to decisions. These questions make them think. If we can get them to think, we can hold their attention.

Question #1: "What would you really like?"

Now our prospects can tell us their goals. Maybe they want softer skin. More energy. A second income so that they can send their children to private school. A chance to change careers. A better holiday experience.

Allow our prospects to describe exactly what they want. This helps them see themselves enjoying these things. And if we can't get them to talk for very long, we can say little things to prompt them such as, "Tell me more."

Bonus: When they tell us what they really like, we know exactly what to offer them.

Question #2: "What will having this do for you?"

Now our prospects experience the feeling they will have if their goals are accomplished. The better they feel at this moment, the more motivated they will be to buy or join. We can see a smile on their faces as they imagine this future good experience.

Question #3: "What would you be willing to do to make this happen?"

Our prospects' answers tell us their commitment levels. We see which sacrifices they will make to create this reality. Maybe a time commitment, or even a money commitment. But the most important thing is, they are willing to take action.

Question #4: "Would you allow me to help you achieve this goal?"

Wow. A powerful and safe question that makes our prospects feel great. When we offer to help, they feel more confident that their goal can be reached. They appreciate that we volunteered to help them, as they may not know what to do next.

Question #5: "Which steps have you already planned?"

"Which steps?" If our prospects are like most people, they have no plan. Most people wish, hope, and dream, but never create a plan to reach their goals. Now our prospects think, "I don't have a plan. I sure hope you have a plan. That would help a lot."

We look like the hero because not only do we have a plan, we will help them with the plan.

Here is a quick sample of using these five questions in conversation.

Question #1: "What would you really like?"

Prospects: "We want to work out of our home."

Question #2: "What will having this do for you?"

Prospects: "By the time we get home from work, it is already 6:15 PM. Then we have to pick up our children from daycare. Then we feed them and put them to bed. We don't have any family time."

Question #3: "What would you be willing to do to make this happen?"

Prospects: "We don't know. Never thought about it. But we know we will have to do something different. We want a change. We don't know what to do."

Question #4: "Would you allow me to help you to achieve this goal?"

Prospects: "Yes! Please help. We could use all the help we can get."

Question #5: "Which steps have you already planned?"

Prospects: "Well, we tried to cut our budget so only one of us would have to work. But the bills piled up, and now we have huge credit card debt. We can't do that again."

As we can see, this is going to be easy. Now we have open-minded prospects ready for our upcoming solution.

Can we go deeper?

Yes. Instead of talking about what they want, we could talk about their problems. People are ten times more interested in problems than benefits. The purpose of business is to solve other people's problems.

So, let's take the problem approach to kick-start the conversation. What kinds of questions would we use? Try these.

Question #1: "What do you think the real problem is?"

Now our prospects have to think about the causes of their problem. Are they engaged? Absolutely.

Question #2: "Has this caused a problem already?"

Our prospects begin to think about the pain of their current situation. Maybe the struggle at the end of the month when the paycheck does not go far enough. Or, trying endless diets that don't work and feeling frustrated.

The more painful the problem, the more motivation to solve it.

Question #3: "Have you tried to fix this problem already? Which solutions have you tried?"

It is good to find out the history of the problem, and which solutions have not worked. Our prospects may have a bias against one of our possible solutions. A good time to find that out is right now. When we hear their struggles with solutions that did not work, we should take mental notes. This will help us avoid objections when we present our solutions.

Question #4: "How much time and effort are you willing to invest to fix this problem?"

We didn't mention money, but that is implied. Most serious prospects know it takes time, money, effort, the cooperation of others, and more to fix their problems. This conversation is becoming very interesting for our prospects.

We help them focus on this problem. Why is this important? Because we hate pain. When we think about a problem, our minds want to think about something else. We want to keep our prospects' attention on the problem.

Question #5: "Is this the biggest problem, or are there more?"

Surprise, surprise. Sometimes our prospects hold back and don't tell us the real problem. We have to build their trust through questions like this before they will tell us the real problem.

Once they divulge the real problem to us, there is a sense of bonding. We will have their undivided attention and trust.

Now for a quick sample conversation.

Question #1: "What do you think the real problem is?"

Prospects: "We don't have enough money. Our salaries are too low."

Question #2: "Has this caused a problem already?"

Prospects: "Sure. Our credit card minimum payments are now over $500 a month. This makes it even harder to pay our mortgage and car payments."

Question #3: "Have you tried to fix this problem already? Which solutions have you tried?"

Prospects: "We both tried to get part-time jobs. But we get home too late and no one local needs part-time help that late in the evening."

Question #4: "How much time and effort are you willing to invest to fix this problem?"

Prospects: "We can work a few hours in the evening, but it has to be after 7 PM."

Question #5: "Is this the biggest problem, or are there more?"

Prospects: "We both hate our jobs. No chance of a raise or promotion. We need new careers where we could earn what we are worth."

What do we think? Will this be an easy conversation about our business? Yes.

Do we need a simpler way to do this? If so, here is a great shortcut.

"Do you think your current plan is the answer?"

A great question to ask our prospects. Why?

#1. They have to stop and think. We have their attention.

#2. This question creates doubt in their minds and makes them question if they have the right plan. Once we create doubt, prospects will look for alternatives and pay attention to our solution.

As humans, most of our plans don't work. Why? Because we feel that we have unlimited willpower, we act logically, and our motivation will last forever. Oh my! With that as our premise, we can see why our current plans will fail. Let's take a look at an example.

John's current diet plan.

- Wake up one hour earlier every morning.

- Exercise briskly for 45 minutes.

- Eat two tablespoons of grass picked from the front lawn.

- Turn down donuts and free snacks at work.

- Drink 10 glasses of lemon juice and water before lunch.

- Walk 45 minutes during lunch to kill the hunger pains.

- Look at pictures of celery for the mid-afternoon snack.

- Swallow two chunks of tasteless baked protein for dinner.

- Watch the family enjoy dessert.

- Replace television with exercise videos.

- Use earplugs to dampen the stomach growling noises at night.

Oh yeah. That's never going to work!

So we ask John, "Do you think your current plan is the answer?" What happens?

John looks at his current failed plan and says, "I am listening. What do you suggest?"

Do humans have lots of plans? Yes. Here are a few.

- Exercise plans.

- Vacation plans.

- Retirement savings plans.

- Projects for the home.

- Better health plans.

- And yes, dieting plans.

There are more plans, but we get the idea. Most of our plans will fail, and we know it. When someone asks us if our current plan is the answer, we are ready to talk.

Everyone should know and use these magic phrases.

These common phrases make it easier to keep our listeners involved.

Let's start with one of the most versatile phrases that we can use anywhere.

"Most people."

Why does this work so well? Because people feel safe when they are with most people. If we are alone, the risk is greater. There is no one else to help us.

Big groups make fun of and criticize loners. We have a program that tells us to fit in with the group. This program is strong.

Where do we get this program? Thousands of years ago we banded together in groups to survive a very hostile world. Lots of larger mammals wanted to eat us. If we got pushed out of the group, rejected by the majority, there was a good chance we would become tiger food. That is why we have a natural tendency to want to fit in with the larger group.

Do we hate criticism? Of course. If we go out as a loner, and make a bad decision, the larger group loves to make fun of us. That is why it is so hard for people to make a decision to do something different. First, there is the chance of criticism. Second, we are unsure of the results. This creates a huge fear of change.

The words "most people" come to the rescue. When our prospects hear these words, they feel safe to make the change we propose. They feel that they are still part of a larger group and their security issues go away.

If team members are skeptical about using magic words, ask them to do this experiment. For the next week, try using the words "most people" every chance they have. They will experience smiles from relaxed prospects.

The words "most people" are covered in detail in other Big Al books. Here are a few examples of using "most people" when presenting to prospects.

"Most people like this part best."

"Most people want an extra paycheck."

"Most people want their face to be their best first impression."

"Most people feel that growing old really hurts."

"Most people want better holidays."

"Most people want more time with their children."

"Most people hate dieting."

"Most people know that dieting doesn't work. They want a better solution."

"Most people can't save enough for retirement."

"Most people want to pay less for their utilities."

"Most people want to fix this problem now."

"Most people don't want to feel bad because they didn't take advantage of an opportunity."

The words "most people" feel natural. They don't scare the people we talk to, and we feel great saying them.

"Everybody knows" and "Everybody says."

The words "everybody knows" and "everybody says" have the same effect. Prospects simply nod in agreement when we say them. These magic words save us time. Why? Because we do not have to spend time on proof. The words we say next are usually accepted as true. No further proof needed. We save time. Our prospects save time. It is a win-win for everyone.

It doesn't take much imagination to come up with some examples. Here are a few to help us get started.

"Everybody knows that toxins are bad for our health."

"Everybody says it is hard to live on one paycheck now."

"Everybody knows it is hard to fit exercise into our daily schedule."

"Everybody says they want to retire early."

"Everybody knows that nothing will change unless **we** change."

"Everybody says that magic words are easy to learn."

"Everybody knows" and "everybody says" are easy, natural magic words that anyone can use immediately.

"There is an old saying …"

No one questions "old sayings." We think, "Old sayings have been around forever. I guess they must be true."

So what would stop us from making up our own "old sayings" whenever we needed them? Nothing.

Imagine we have a message that our prospects resist. We could help our message get inside our prospects' heads by making it part of an old saying. Here is an example.

We say, "This super-nutrition pill will make your face appear younger." A great message, but it gets blocked by our prospects' minds.

Instead, we rephrase this by saying, "There is an old saying that the best way to prevent wrinkles is from the inside." Now our super-nutrition pill must be a great solution in their minds.

Another example?

We say, "Our business will give you a second source of income. You don't have to worry that all of your income depends on the mood of your boss." While this sounds good, our prospects might still be skeptical. Let's rephrase this again using these magic words.

"There is an old saying that we can sleep better at night when we have two paychecks instead of one."

Of course this must be true because it is an old saying. Now we deliver the message that having a second source of income is safer than hoping the one income doesn't go away.

Let's do one more example.

We say, "We don't sell diet products. We sell a lifestyle change." Pretty uninspiring. Our prospects' minds drift to something else.

Instead we say, "There is an old saying that if you go on a diet, then you will eventually have to get off the diet. We prevent weight from coming back with our no-diet system."

Old sayings feel like a summary. Prospects like the shorter message.

"Would it be okay if ...?"

This is one of our favorites. Why? Not only does it get our prospects' attention by politely asking permission, but it also commands them to think, "Yes! Yes! Yes! I want to help you in any way possible."

Now, we could say, "Would you? Could you? Can you?" But those words don't have the same power. These five powerful words should be a habit. Whenever we catch ourselves asking for a favor, permission, or decision without saying these words, we should slap ourselves on the wrist! It may take a while to make these words a habit, but these words will serve us for the rest of our lives.

These five words are great opening words. Why? They are rejection-free. They are polite. Here are some examples.

"Would it be okay if we look at this right now?"

"Would it be okay if we talked more about this during our coffee break?"

"Would it be okay if we have a cup of coffee with Mary? She could tell us what she is doing to replace her job."

"Would it be okay if you try this diet for seven days? See how easy it is to lose weight when you are not hungry."

"Would it be okay if we look at another option?"

"Would it be okay if I showed you what I am doing?"

These five words are great closing words also. Let's look at some possibilities.

"Would it be okay if we got started now?"

"Would it be okay if we called your best friend first?"

"Would it be okay if you tried these products first?"

"Would it be okay if we started now to stop those wrinkles?"

"Would it be okay if we got online now and spent five minutes lowering your electricity bill?"

"Would it be okay if you drank this every afternoon and had more energy?"

"Would it be okay if we planned your next family vacation right now?"

"Would it be okay if you never had to worry about getting ripped off again?"

You might be thinking these words sound familiar. Why? Because others use these words to get "yes" decisions from us daily.

Think about children. Small, powerless, but they get everything they want. How do they do it? Magic words, of course. See if these requests from our children sound familiar.

"Would it be okay if I did my homework on Sunday night instead?"

"Would it be okay if I stayed at Heather's house tonight?"

"Would it be okay if I borrowed the family car and never brought it back?" (Yes, my daughter got away with that.)

So, would it be okay if we added "Would it be okay if …" to our magic words toolbox? It works. All we have to do is to use these words.

Let's take the next few magic phrases and put them into a practical situation that we all encounter.

"What do you do for a living?"

Imagine someone asks us what we do for a living. Here is the perfect chance to deliver our message, if we use the right technique. Our prospects expect a one-sentence answer. However, with magic words, we can buy more attention time in our prospects' minds.

First, let's look at an ordinary answer.

Prospects: "What do you do for a living?"

Us: "I sell products for the XYZ company."

Okay, accurate. Exciting? No. Our prospecting chances are pretty low.

Let's see how that sounds with a proven ice breaker.

Prospects: "What do you do for a living?"

Us: "I show people how to start a part-time business so they have extra money."

Better. We delivered our benefit message inside of our prospects' minds. But could we do better? Yes! Let's upgrade to a problem/solution answer.

Prospects: "What do you do for a living?"

Us: "Well, you know how things are so expensive now? I show people how to have a second paycheck so that they won't stress about money."

Mention a problem, and then our solution feels better for our prospects. But we only get a sentence or two. What if we wanted to take control of our prospects' minds for longer than that? How can we get and hold our prospects' attention for several sentences?

The answer is with a story.

Everyone has time for a story. Humans love stories. Young children, as soon as they can talk will say, "Mommy! Daddy! Please tell me a story."

Stories mesmerize humans, and we listen longer as a result.

So how will we announce to our prospects that we are going to tell them a story? We could use the words, "Once upon a time," but we usually reserve those words for children's stories. Instead, we need a different phrase to put our prospects' minds into story mode. Here it is:

"Suppose that ..."

These two words will kickstart our prospects' imaginations. They will make a movie out of the words that follow.

We like communicating with stories. It is a natural way for humans to think, understand, and learn. Listening to stories is easy. We've been listening to stories all our lives.

Stories can be short or long. But we will only have the benefits of freezing our prospects' brains for a few seconds. That means our stories must be short. The good news is that short stories can be several sentences long. This gives our message more depth and excitement.

Here are some examples:

Prospects: "What do you do for a living?"

Us: "Suppose that you come back from lunch and feel like taking a nap. You say to yourself, 'This is no fun. I hate struggling every afternoon like this. I wonder if there is anything I can do to have healthy energy instead of drowning myself in caffeine?' Well, I have something for that."

Bam! Our complete message, delivered in a story. What is extra nice is that our prospects will remember our story. Every time they feel tired, they will remember our story. It is like having an automatic follow-up alarm inside their heads. The human mind wants to believe stories, and is wired to remember them.

No rejection. Just a simple story answer to the question, "What do you do for a living?"

What made this all possible? The magic words, "Suppose that …" This turns on the movie projector inside our prospects' minds.

Here are some "Suppose that …" stories to prompt our imaginations.

Prospects: "What do you do for a living?"

Us: "Suppose that you look into the mirror one morning and say to yourself, 'I want my skin to look younger. I don't like these fine wrinkles. I loved how my skin was radiant when I was a teenager. I wonder if there is something I can do without surgery or Botox.' Well, I show women how to put youth back into their skin by simply changing their skincare products."

Prospects: "What do you do for a living?"

Us: "Suppose that you wake up one morning and think, 'I like my home and my family. I hate leaving for work in the morning and fighting traffic. I waste two hours every day in bumper-to-bumper traffic feeling stressed. What would life be like if I could work out of my home? No more stressful commute, and I could be with my family.' Well, I show people how to make this dream come true."

Prospects: "What do you do for a living?"

Us: "Suppose that we wanted to live longer instead of dying quickly. What would we do to make that happen? Of course we would exercise every day and eat well. But instead of taking one-size-fits-all vitamins and minerals, which nutrients would we take that could extend our lives? We don't know. And that is a problem for most people. I show people exactly which nutrients they can take to live better and longer."

Prospects: "What do you do for a living?"

Us: "Suppose that you get an electricity bill every month. You think to yourself, 'Summer starts next month. My air conditioning costs will be through the roof. Every summer my electricity bill triples. What can I do?' Well, I help people lower their electricity rates so they can enjoy their summers instead of sweating."

If we get bored with saying "Suppose that," we could substitute, "Imagine that." The word "imagine" also turns on the movie projector in our prospects' minds. And yes, this tells our prospects that a story is coming.

Here is an example from Paul Fillare, who sells legal services.

Prospects: "What do you do for a living?"

Paul: "Imagine that you get into an argument with your landlord because he won't fix anything he said he would. Your dry cleaners ruin your favorite shirt, and they have a 'not responsible for ruined items' sign. You get a speeding ticket when you know that you weren't speeding. Or you become a victim of identity theft. Well, I help make all of those situations disappear, like they never happened."

Want another example?

Prospects: "What do you do for a living?"

Us: "So imagine it is time for the family vacation. You think, 'Where should we go this year? Airfares and hotels are so expensive. We can't go far. But, we do need a break.' Well, I help families get five-star holidays for the price of an average hotel. Now their vacations create lifelong memories."

"Here is the short story."

"Suppose that" and "Imagine that" aren't the only ways to signal to our prospects that we are about to tell them a story. This phrase is even more direct: "Here is the short story." There is no doubt in our prospects' minds that we will be telling them a story. But it is okay. They love stories. And they love short. Everyone is busy. When we promise that our story will be short, they will listen.

Here are some more examples to answer the "What do you do for a living?" question.

"Here is the short story. Do you get an electricity bill? Ask yourself, 'Would it be okay if my electricity bill was lower and I could spend the savings on something I enjoy?' That is what we do. Now, ask yourself if your neighbors would love you more if you allow them to save money too. Of course they would! By doing this, you will earn money every time your neighbors turn on their lights."

There it is. Our entire message delivered in a few seconds. Our prospects hear our message, and can decide if our message will serve them or not.

Another example? Let's do a few.

"Here is the short story. Jobs interfere with our week. Not only do they take eight hours of our time each day, but the grind of commuting makes it even worse. When we finally get home to see our family, we feel exhausted. So I offer people a chance to work out of their homes with their own home-based business. A lot of people like that option."

Our prospects will hear this story and decide if that is a good option for them, or not.

"Here is the short story. You deserve a raise. It is easier to get that raise with your own part-time business."

What do you think our prospects will ask us next? It is nice when prospects ask us for more information about our business.

Let's try a diet product example.

"Here is the short story. People exercise, starve themselves, eat funny foods, and the weight keeps coming back. Going on a diet means eventually having to go off the diet. Then the weight comes back with a few extra pounds to punish us for trying. I show people how to lose weight by never going on a diet. Instead they simply change what they have for breakfast."

Skincare?

"Here is the short story. Wrinkles will come. We can't avoid them. But, we can put them off an extra 15 or 20 years with the right skincare. I show women how to get the right skincare."

Natural cleaners?

"Here is the short story. Everyone wants to help the environment, but we don't have time to pick up trash out of our rivers and lakes. But, we can help our environment even more by switching to natural-based cleaners instead of the chemicals we use today. I help people make that switch."

Health products?

"Here is the short story. We will die, but there is no need to rush that. So we ask ourselves, 'What can I do to extend my life?' I help people with this."

Prospects love it when we say, "Here is the short story." It lets them know that we won't take up much of their time.

Utility bills?

"Here is the short story. You get an electricity bill. You might as well pay a lower rate."

Cellphones?

"Here is the short story. You pay your cellphone bill every month. You might as well pay less."

Ready to focus on some magic phrases for closing our prospects?

CLOSING AND GETTING THE DECISION.

Our biggest obstacle to getting a decision?

Procrastination.

It is easy to **not** make a decision. It takes no effort. We can delay our commitment to action forever. It sounds like this.

"I need to think it over."

"We will get back to you."

"I need to research this more."

"We are not ready to start yet."

"Let me ask my friends first."

"My spouse and I need to talk it over more."

"I haven't had a chance to look at it yet."

"Is there a video or more information you could send me?"

We hear these delays, give up, and hope we get an "I tried my best" bonus from our company. Companies don't pay these bonuses in their compensation plan.

We only get paid for "yes" decisions.

So let's try some magic words and phrases to guide our prospects to faster decisions.

"Choosing."

When we start our business, we make up or guess what to say to our prospects.

Our reasoning? "Oh, it just feels good. I had a hunch this might be something to try. My new plan is random guessing." Ugh! This may not be the best way to build a solid future business.

Let's compare and see the difference better, more professional phrases make.

> Amateur distributor using hunches: "Uh, so what did you like best about what I showed you? Would you like to join? My sponsor made a lot of money. We are unique. Come on, why not give it a go?"

> Professional distributor using better phrases: "Choosing to move forward is a choice. Choosing not to move forward is also a choice."

When we use the word "choosing," some good things happen.

First, our prospects feel that they are in control. Their fear of us pushing a decision on them goes away. When our prospects relax, they can make a better decision for their needs.

Second, when our prospects "choose," they make their final decision. We don't have to worry about them delaying things by saying, "I want to think it over."

Third, no chance of rejection. All we do is allow our prospects to choose the action that is best for them. If they choose to move forward with us, great. If they choose not to move forward, that is great also. That might be what is best for them.

Here is the good news. We can use sound bites and other more advanced techniques to make our choice the best choice ever! No selling or convincing. Prospects are smart. They have common sense. They can figure out what is best for them. They will choose us and our options.

Here is what that looks like in action.

Etienne Laliberté tells his prospects, "Choosing to slow down the aging process with these supplements is a good choice. But you can also choose not to invest in your health and keep your current aging speed."

The prospects think, "What??? Keep my current aging speed? No. No. No. Give me those supplements!"

Let's do more examples.

"Choosing to start our diet program now is a great choice. And choosing to keep your current weight by not starting our diet program is also a choice."

"Choosing to start building your part-time business tonight is a choice you can make now. But, you can also make a choice not to start, and settle for your current commute to your job until you retire."

"Choosing to step out and become your own boss is a choice. However, you can also choose not to do this and continue to work for someone else."

"Choosing a dream vacation with us is a choice your family will love. But, you can also choose to continue taking your vacations the same way you did last year."

"Choosing to join our business and learn new skills is a choice. But you can also choose to stay where you are."

Our prospects feel good. We put them in control. Don't worry, though. When we show our prospects the real options, most will want our solutions.

"So what is going to be easier for you?"

Say these words: "So what is going to be easier for you?" Then, give our prospects two options.

Option #1. Continue life as it is. Yes, that is making a decision not to do anything. But, notice that this **is** a decision.

Option #2. Take action on our message. This would be a decision to buy or join.

Here are those closing words in action:

"So what is going to be easier for you? To continue fighting traffic every day for the rest of your working career? Or, to get started tonight to begin the countdown to firing your boss, so that you can work out of your home?"

No more procrastination. Our prospects must decide if they want to take no action, give up hope, and resign themselves to a lifetime of miserable commuting in traffic ... or, to take action now, so that they will have a different future.

Easy. No rejection. Done.

Want more examples?

"So what is going to be easier for you? To take good care of your skin now, or to have to resort to Botox injections later?"

"So what is going to be easier for you? To continue taking your holidays at your mother-in-law's apartment? Or to have a real family vacation by using our discount travel services?"

"So what is going to be easier for you? To ask your boss for a 50% raise, or to start your part-time business now and get the money you need?"

"So what is going to be easier for you? To feel embarrassed that you are paying the highest electricity rates on your street? Or, for us to spend five minutes online now to set up your lower rate?"

"So what is going to be easier for you? To continue dieting, exercising, eating funny foods, and watching the weight keep coming back? Or, to drink our weight-loss protein shake every morning, and never worry about dieting again?"

"So what is going to be easier for you? To continue fighting this traffic every day until you are 65 years old? Or, to start your part-time business tonight so next year you can work out of your home?"

"So what is going to be easier for you? To continue to try to get by on one paycheck? Or, to start a part-time business so you will have extra money?"

These words create clear choices for our prospects.

"This either works for you or not. So what do you want to do?"

Here is another way to give our prospects a choice. When they make their choice, there is no more procrastination. Now for some quick examples.

"Having an extra paycheck either works for you or not. So what do you want to do?"

"Losing weight by changing what you have for breakfast either works for you or not. So what do you want to do?"

"Being your own boss instead of taking orders from someone else either works for you or not. So what do you want to do?"

"Having younger-looking skin either works for you or not. So what do you want to do?"

"Getting paid what you are worth either works for you are not. So what do you want to do?"

"Reducing your risk by having a second paycheck either works for you or not. So what do you want to do?"

"Having a chance to win fully-paid holidays either works for you or not. So what do you want to do?"

"Making your electricity bill smaller by going online for five minutes either works for you or not. So what do you want to do?"

Prospects love choices. They feel in control. Why not take the pressure off our prospects by allowing them to choose what is best for them?

Want another way to take the pressure off our prospects? We could rephrase their choices by saying this:

"You can make a decision to start today, or you can make a decision not to start today and keep your life exactly as it is."

The choice is clear.

"How will you feel when …?"

It is easy to keep our prospects' attention when they are doing the talking. Prospects love to talk about themselves. When we listen to them, we build a stronger rapport. People like people who listen.

We get our prospects to talk by asking questions. But the types of questions we ask will make a difference. We don't want to ask prospects questions with simple "yes" or "no" answers. Instead, we will ask open-ended questions that get our prospects to talk longer.

We can go a step further. What if our question got our prospects to visualize the benefits of our offer? It is easier for prospects to buy when they can see themselves using the product or enjoying the benefits of our opportunity. We've probably all heard someone say, "I don't see myself doing this." That means they can't visualize this ever happening to them. This leads to a "no" decision.

Here is the question we can use to get this visualization going:

"How will you feel when …?"

This question turns on the movie projector in their minds. Here is an example.

"How will you feel when you step in front of the mirror, wearing your high school clothes from years ago?"

Our prospect visualizes a thinner, fitter body in front of the mirror. A smile begins. They're practically selling themselves now.

Here are some more examples of this powerful question.

"How will you feel when you walk into your boss' office and tell your boss that you cannot fit him into your schedule any longer?"

"How will you feel when you realize that you are the youngest-looking attendee at your 20-year high school class reunion?"

"How will you feel when your entire family sits down at this all-inclusive resort to eat, and you don't have to worry about the restaurant bill?"

"How will you feel when you step on the bathroom scale and notice that you've lost 10 pounds already?"

"How will you feel when you tell your children this year's vacation will be at Disney World?"

"How will you feel when you tell your difficult landlord, 'Just a moment. Let me get my lawyer on the phone.'"

"How will you feel when you can sleep in until 7:30 every morning because you don't have to fight commuter traffic any longer?"

"How will you feel when you know you are earning a bonus check every time your neighbors turn on their lights?"

The earlier in our conversation that we can introduce this question, the more effective it becomes. Why? When they see themselves enjoying our offer in their minds ... well, that is where their decisions are made!

Our prospects make decisions based on their feelings. Later, they justify their decisions with logic.

"Does it make sense ..."

Green personalities are the analytical people we meet. You can find these people in professions such as programming, accounting, and engineering. Want to get green personalities to make a decision? Use this question.

"Does it make sense for you to do this?"

We are not pushing them into a corner, forcing them to make a "yes" or "no" decision. Instead, we are only asking if it makes sense. That is a huge difference to a green personality. They won't feel pressured.

Here are a few examples.

> "Does it make sense to get started now, so you can get your first check next week?"

> "Does it make sense for us to start the detox cleanse as accountability partners?"

> "Does it make sense to order a two-month supply now?"

> "Does it make sense to stop hoping for a 50% pay raise?"

> "Does it make sense to add a second income to make retirement easier?"

"If ... if not."

Somehow the "if" word grabs our attention. Maybe we feel something bad is going to happen to us, but "if" means we can do something about it. Regardless, the "if" word is fun to use because it works.

Here are some examples of using this formula.

"If going to work, paying the bills, and saving the leftovers works for you ... great. If not, let's talk."

"If working for your boss, commuting, and getting a few weeks of vacation every year works for you ... great. If not, we should talk."

"If dieting, exercise, and eating funny food works for you ... great. If not, use our breakfast shake to lose those extra pounds."

"If you can tolerate rip-offs and being taken advantage of ... no problem. If not, use our legal plan."

"If letting your skin dry out from the inside works for you ... no problem. If not, use this every night before bedtime."

"If ordinary vacations are fine ... no problem. If not, check this out."

Not only do we grab our prospects' attention, we close and get decisions instantly.

"Do we want to risk doing nothing?"

We don't want to be aggressive or high-pressure. But, doing nothing is a decision to stay exactly where we are. There are risks if we don't make changes in our lives. Part of our message should be to let our prospects know not only the rewards, but also the risks. As we can see, the word "risk" triggers our prospects' attention.

Everyone wants to avoid risk. Why? Because we have a tremendous fear of loss. There is an old saying that our fear of loss is greater than our desire for gain.

Our mission is to deliver our message to open minds. Then our prospects can decide if our message will serve them or not. The key word here is "decide." Our prospects must make a decision to move forward, or to stay where they are.

To do this we will re-frame our prospects' view of risk. We will let them know that there is risk going forward, of course. But, we will also let our prospects know that it could be risky to stay where they are.

Now we will cushion this question by including us in the question. Then it does not sound as aggressive or scary. Here are a few examples.

> "Do we want to risk our financial future by having all of our income in one place?"

> "What will happen to our skin if we don't protect it from wrinkles?"

> "What will happen if we don't go on a diet and begin to lose weight?"

> "How will we deal with increasing prices if we don't have a second income?"

We can put these words into our normal presentation. See if this would get our prospects' attention.

"You don't have to take advantage of our business. But, you might be thinking, 'If I don't join this business, how risky is it to depend on my boss for huge raises so I can make ends meet?'"

Another way of verbalizing this? We could say, "So what's going to happen to people who decide to risk everything on their one income from their job? I will let you take that risk if you decide to limit your income sources."

Ouch!

Now, we have our prospects thinking about our offer. Our message was heard.

"Are you married to your job, or are you open-minded?"

I like this phrase because it helps close our prospects before we even begin our presentation.

Twenty years ago, Jean-Philippe Hulin and I were conducting a workshop in Belgium. While eating lunch, we noticed that the waiter was extremely busy. He stopped at our table and Jean-Philippe said, "Are you married to your job, or are you open-minded?"

The waiter replied, "Open-minded! My coworker did not show up for work today. I am doing two jobs. Plus, I won't get off work today at 5 PM like I planned. Because my coworker did not show up, I have to work until 8 PM. Yes, I am open-minded!"

We told the waiter that we would talk to him later in the afternoon when we finished our workshop. We knew he was busy.

We took a mid-afternoon coffee break. The waiter came to our table and said, "You won't forget me, will you? I am looking forward to talking with you."

Why was this so easy?

First, most people don't want to say, "I am closed-minded." It is easy to get "yes" answers when we ask, "Are you open-minded?"

Second, so many people are dissatisfied with their jobs. They want more in their lives, but don't know where to find it. They are happy to hear that we can give them one more option for their lives.

Think about the people who reply, "No, I am not open-minded. I am happy with my job. I don't want to look at anything else." These non-prospects saved us time and saved themselves time by telling us that they didn't want to look now.

Let's do a few more examples using this approach.

"Are you open-minded about some new career possibilities?"

"Are you open-minded about a new way to lose weight?"

"Are you open-minded about some new skincare options?"

"Do you feel open-minded when it comes to shopping for new products?"

"Here is the bottom line."

In financial reports, most people see a blur of numbers. The number that stands out is the last line, the bottom line. That last line shows if the business made money, or lost money. In other words, it is the shortcut or summary of the entire report.

When we say "Here is the bottom line" to prospects, their ears perk up. Their minds are thinking, "Great. This is all I need to know. Give it to me now."

This is another great place to put our sales message. We have our prospects' full attention. Let's do some quick examples.

"Here is the bottom line. If we don't start our own business, then we are sentencing ourselves to a lifetime of labor."

"Here is the bottom line. Never go on a diet. Why? Because when you get off the diet, the weight will come screaming back."

"Here is the bottom line. Nobody is going to get a 50% pay raise this year. We have to do something on our own to get ahead."

"Here is the bottom line. We want to live longer. This can help."

"Here is the bottom line. We eat junk food, and that makes us feel like junk."

"Here is the bottom line. It can take years to get a promotion. However, you can promote yourself as fast as you want in our business."

"Here is the bottom line. If we keep doing the same things, keep going to the same job, nothing is going to change."

"Here is the bottom line. At 50 years old, you can't save enough money to retire. You need a second income."

"Here is the bottom line. You can continue paying more for your family holidays, or you can save huge money by booking them with us."

If we started our presentation with the "bottom line," most prospects, especially the red personalities, would love us.

"Are you okay with ...?"

We talk about this powerful four-word phrase in our books, *Pre-Closing For Network Marketing* and *Closing For Network Marketing*.

Saying this powerful four-word phrase gets our prospects' instant attention. They stop and think, "I am about to lose something. I don't like losing things. I have a fear of missing out. What is it? Tell me now!" And now we insert our message past all the barriers that block communication to our prospects' minds.

We can use this phrase early in our conversations with prospects. Here are some examples.

"Are you okay with this long commute to work every day for the rest of your career?"

"Are you okay with not having enough extra money to fund your retirement?"

"Are you okay with working 45 years like your parents?"

"Are you okay with starving yourself and dieting, only to see the weight come back when you stop?"

"Are you okay with doing nothing to stop the wrinkles from forming?"

"Are you okay with showing your children pictures of Disney World, instead of taking them there?"

"Are you okay with working 40 hours every week to build your boss's dream, and having no time for your own dreams?"

"Are you okay with leaving the children at daycare while you go to work?"

"Are you okay with having no defense when other people try to take advantage of you?"

"Are you okay with giving up on your dreams and staying here at this job?"

"Are you okay with feeling tired and grumpy every day when you come home from work?"

"Are you okay with feeling old and not doing anything about it?"

As we see, this phrase creates instant pain – and therefore instant decisions - within our prospects' minds. Now they pay attention. They don't want the results of doing nothing.

But we can also use this phrase at the end of our presentations. Some examples?

"Are you okay with just giving up and not even trying this?" (Okay, a little aggressive, but the choice is clear.)

"Are you okay with not trying to fix this problem?"

"Are you okay with continuing ordinary diets that don't work?"

"Are you okay with not using the skin serum and allowing your skin to continue to age?"

"Are you okay with not having the extra money and watching television instead?"

"Are you okay with continuing to put off the decision to fix this problem?"

"Are you okay with continuing to have age take its toll on you?"

"Are you okay with working at a job that you have no patience for?"

"Are you okay with not getting online now and fixing your electricity overcharges?"

These four words get our prospects to clear their minds and make a decision. When our decisions are hard and painful, we lose attention and think of something more pleasant. These four words prevent that.

Mind-reading magic words.

Great things happen when we perform our mind-reading skills.

First, when we read our prospects' minds, we create better rapport. They feel that we understand them. They think, "You and I think the same." This is good. We remove much of the doubt and skepticism they may have about us and our message.

Second, this is impressive. We look like we have superpowers. This gives us more influence and impact with our message.

So let's open up our prospects' minds with these mind-reading magic words.

"As you probably know."

Well, if they already know what we are about to say, it must be true. This means we can bypass the charts, proof, and endless details. This allows us to deliver a clear message. Some examples?

"As you probably know, commuting to work steals time from our family."

"As you probably know, losing weight is very difficult."

"As you probably know, wrinkles won't go away on their own."

"As you probably know, jobs interfere with our week."

"As you probably know, a second income will fast-track us to retirement."

"As you probably know, family vacations are expensive."

By adding the words "as you probably know" to our facts, we make the facts more believable. What a nice way to get our message across to prospects.

"If you are like most people."

Well, most people are like most people. And, most people want to be like others. Why? Because we know that it's safer to be in a group. We don't have to think so hard about our choices if others have made the same choices first.

Let's do some quick examples.

"If you are like most people, you want to send your children to better schools."

"If you are like most people, you want to lose weight but not feel starved."

"If you are like most people, a second paycheck every month would make things a lot easier."

"If you are like most people, you might have dreams about being your own boss."

"If you are like most people, you want to put off wrinkles as long as possible."

"If you are like most people, getting a 50% raise is unlikely."

"If you are like most people, you notice things are more expensive now."

This phrase helps our prospects agree to our opening facts. Then, we can move on with the rest of our message.

As we see, "If you are like most people" is a very powerful phrase. Why?

As we know, decisions can be hard. Thinking, considering, and weighing the options sucks the energy out of our brains. To save energy, our brains look for shortcuts.

One of the shortcuts is to see what other people have done before us. That is why reviews are important in the decision-making process. When confronted with too many options, our brains look for an easy way out. Our brains say, "Let's do what most other people did in a similar situation."

We feel secure by going along with the crowd.

Want to make this feel even more personal?

Then substitute this phrase instead: "If you are like me ..." Here are some quick examples.

"If you are like me, you hate commuting."

"If you are like me, you find it hard to set aside time for exercise."

"If you are like me, you hate it when people take advantage of us."

"If you are like me, you want your face to be your best first impression."

"You are probably thinking ..."

Well, everybody is always thinking. What we will do next is guess what they are thinking. Don't worry if we are wrong. Why? Because we said "probably" and not certainly. And if we guess right, we look like a genius! Some examples:

"You are probably thinking, 'Do I have to be a salesman?'"

"You are probably thinking, 'How much is this going to cost me?'"

"You are probably thinking, 'Where will I find people to talk to?'"

"You are probably thinking, 'How will I know if this works or not?'"

"You are probably thinking, 'Is it really possible to work out of my home instead?'"

"You are probably thinking, 'Is there some sort of guarantee?'"

"You are probably thinking, 'What do I have to do to earn that money?'"

This phrase helps us bond with our prospects. They feel that we have empathy for their situation.

Another way of saying this would be, "You might be wondering." Either phrase works. Let's use what feels more natural for us.

FINALLY ...

The first few seconds are critical.

We have one chance to capture our prospects' attention. Can we do it?

Yes.

If we fail, our message goes unheard.

Choosing to use these magic words will brighten our futures. More people will hear and engage with our wonderful messages.

So ...

If talking to zoned-out zombies works for you ... great. If not, use these magic phrases and watch your business grow.

THANK YOU.

Thank you for purchasing and reading this book. We hope you found some ideas that will work for you.

Before you go, would it be okay if we asked a small favor? Would you take just one minute and leave a sentence or two reviewing this book online? Your review can help others choose what they will read next. It would be greatly appreciated by many fellow readers.

I travel the world 240+ days each year.
Let me know if you want me to stop in your
area and conduct a live Big Al training.

BigAlSeminars.com

FREE Big Al Training Audios
Magic Words for Prospecting
plus Free eBook and the Big Al Report!

BigAlBooks.com/free

More Big Al Books

Mini-Scripts for the Four Color Personalities
How to Talk to our Network Marketing Prospects

As network marketing leaders, we want to move people to take positive actions. Using their own color language is how we will do it.

Quick Start Guide for Network Marketing
Get Started FAST, Rejection-FREE!

Our new team members are at the peak of their enthusiasm now. Let's give them the fast-start skills to kick-start their business immediately.

The Two-Minute Story for Network Marketing
Create the Big-Picture Story That Sticks!

Worried about presenting your business opportunity to prospects? Here is the solution. The two-minute story is the ultimate presentation to network marketing prospects.

How to Build Your Network Marketing Business in 15 Minutes a Day

Anyone can set aside 15 minutes a day to start building their financial freedom. Of course we would like to have more time, but in just 15 minutes we can change our lives forever.

How to Meet New People Guidebook
Overcome Fear and Connect Now

Meeting new people is easy when we can read their minds. Discover how strangers automatically size us up in seconds, using three basic standards.

How to Meet New People Guidebook
Overcome Fear and Connect Now

Meeting new people is easy when we can read their minds. Discover how strangers automatically size us up in seconds, using three basic standards.

Why Are My Goals Not Working?
Color Personalities for Network Marketing Success

Setting goals that work for us is easy when we have guidelines and a checklist.

Closing for Network Marketing
Getting Prospects Across The Finish Line

Here are 46 years' worth of our best closes. All of these closes are kind and comfortable for prospects, and rejection-free for us.

Pre-Closing for Network Marketing
"Yes" Decisions Before The Presentation

Instead of selling to customers with facts, features and benefits, let's talk to prospects in a way they like. We can now get that "yes" decision first, so the rest of our presentation will be easy.

The One-Minute Presentation
Explain Your Network Marketing Business Like A Pro

Learn to make your business grow with this efficient, focused business presentation technique.

Retail Sales for Network Marketers
How to Get New Customers for Your MLM Business

Learn how to position your retail sales so people are happy to buy. Don't know where to find customers for your products and services? Learn how to market to people who want what you offer.

Getting "Yes" Decisions
What insurance agents and financial advisors can say to clients

In the new world of instant decisions, we need to master the words and phrases to successfully move our potential clients to lifelong clients. Easy … when we can read their minds and service their needs immediately.

3 Easy Habits For Network Marketing
Automate Your MLM Success

Use these habits to create a powerful stream of activity in your network marketing business.

Start SuperNetworking!
5 Simple Steps to Creating Your Own Personal Networking Group

Start your own personal networking group and have new, pre-sold customers and prospects come to you.

The Four Color Personalities for MLM
The Secret Language for Network Marketing

Learn the skill to quickly recognize the four personalities and how to use magic words to translate your message.

Ice Breakers!
How To Get Any Prospect To Beg You For A Presentation

Create unlimited Ice Breakers on-demand. Your distributors will no longer be afraid of prospecting, instead, they will love prospecting.

How To Get Instant Trust, Belief, Influence and Rapport!
13 Ways To Create Open Minds By Talking To The Subconscious Mind

Learn how the pros get instant rapport and cooperation with even the coldest prospects. The #1 skill every new distributor needs.

First Sentences for Network Marketing
How To Quickly Get Prospects On Your Side

Attract more prospects and give more presentations with great first sentences that work.

Motivation. Action. Results.
How Network Marketing Leaders Move Their Teams

Learn the motivational values and triggers our team members have, and learn to use them wisely. By balancing internal motivation and external motivation methods, we can be more effective motivators.

How To Build Network Marketing Leaders
Volume One: Step-By-Step Creation Of MLM Professionals

This book will give you the step-by-step activities to actually create leaders.

How To Build Network Marketing Leaders
Volume Two: Activities And Lessons For MLM Leaders

You will find many ways to change people's viewpoints, to change their beliefs, and to reprogram their actions.

The Complete Three-Book Network Marketing Leadership Series

Series includes: How To Build Network Marketing Leaders Volume One, How To Build Network Marketing Leaders Volume Two, and Motivation. Action. Results.

51 Ways and Places to Sponsor New Distributors
Discover Hot Prospects For Your Network Marketing Business

Learn the best places to find motivated people to build your team and your customer base.

How To Prospect, Sell And Build Your Network Marketing Business With Stories

If you want to communicate effectively, add your stories to deliver your message.

26 Instant Marketing Ideas To Build Your Network Marketing Business

176 pages of amazing marketing lessons and case studies to get more prospects for your business immediately.

Big Al's MLM Sponsoring Magic

How To Build A Network Marketing Team Quickly

This book shows the beginner exactly what to do, exactly what to say, and does it through the eyes of a brand-new distributor.

Public Speaking Magic

Success and Confidence in the First 20 Seconds

By using any of the three major openings in this book, we can confidently start our speeches and presentations without fear.

Worthless Sponsor Jokes

Network Marketing Humor

Here is a collection of worthless sponsor jokes from 25 years of the "Big Al Report." Network marketing can be enjoyable, and we can have fun making jokes along the way.

How To Get Kids To Say Yes!

Using the Secret Four Color Languages to Get Kids to Listen

Turn discipline and frustration into instant cooperation. Kids love to say "yes" when they hear their own color-coded language.

BigAlBooks.com

About the Authors

Keith Schreiter has 20+ years of experience in network marketing and MLM. He shows network marketers how to use simple systems to build a stable and growing business.

So, do you need more prospects? Do you need your prospects to commit instead of stalling? Want to know how to engage and keep your group active? If these are the types of skills you would like to master, you will enjoy his "how-to" style.

Keith speaks and trains in the U.S., Canada, and Europe.

Tom "Big Al" Schreiter has 40+ years of experience in network marketing and MLM. As the author of the original "Big Al" training books in the late '70s, he has continued to speak in over 80 countries on using the exact words and phrases to get prospects to open up their minds and say "YES."

His passion is marketing ideas, marketing campaigns, and how to speak to the subconscious mind in simplified, practical ways. He is always looking for case studies of incredible marketing campaigns that give usable lessons.

As the author of numerous audio trainings, Tom is a favorite speaker at company conventions and regional events.

Printed in Poland
by Amazon Fulfillment
Poland Sp. z o.o., Wrocław

49095340R00065